To Sandy

Blessings

Dr. Sugar Frost

2/22/17

Dr. Sugar Trask

Shattered Mirror

A Life of Despair!

The Introduction

~From Hell to Heaven~

Shattered Mirror

© 2016 Sugar Trask

Printed in the USA

ISBN (Print Version): ISBN-13: 978-0692235089 (Sugar Trask)

ISBN--10:0692235086

Cover design: Shekinah Glory

Publishing

Editor: Shekinah Glory Publishing

Some names and identifying details have been changed to protect the privacy of individuals.

Contact the author

www.scarfree03ministries.com

Dedication

~~~~~~

This book is dedicated to my Father (God) who has blessed me to overcome the obstacles that have been set before me throughout my life. Because of the grace of my Father, I am who I am today.

This book is also dedicated to each of you, my dear brothers and sisters in Christ. Be strong and do not lose heart. Refuse to give up. The enemy would have you believe in hopelessness, but he will not succeed as long as you maintain your position of hope. Give him no ground. Take the time to exercise your faith and believe in God.

For our light affliction, which is but for a moment, is working for us a far more exceeding and eternal weight of glory. 2 Corinthians 4:17

Acknowledgements

~~~~~~~~~~~~~~~~~~~~~~~~~~~~~~~~~

To the children who have been a vital part of my life:

Nitasha Graham

Thomas B. Graham

Kashonda Graham

Tasia Graham

Trenton Graham

Kameron Graham

Za Quiya Graham

Eiycis Graham

Tariq Graham

Olivia Jenkins

Lamar Jenkins

Carmen Jenkins

Shawntel Jenkins

Nireba Graham

Ja Naye Rivers

Phillip Jackson III

Thomas B. Graham III

Endorsements

~~~~~~~~~~~~~~~~~~~~~~~~~~~~~~~~~~~~~~~

We live in an era of rampant immorality, alcoholism and drug addiction. It is a time of unprecedented moral failure and spiritual darkness. Despite all that, God's light revealed through His son Jesus Christ shines brighter than ever and the power of the gospel to save, heal, deliver and restore is just as mighty as it ever was.

In this book *Shattered Mirror: A life of Despair*, evangelist Sugar Trask shares the story of her life as she floundered on the road of life, was broken and finally restored by the power of God. Her life story is also the story of countless thousands who desperately need an encounter with God. Many people you know need this book. Read it, give it away -- and God will use her testimony to save and heal others the same way she was saved and healed.

Joan Hunter
Author
Founder and President of Joan Hunter Ministries

Evangelist Sugar Trask takes us on the very personal and painful journey of her life in her latest book *Shattered Mirror*. Sugar's life is a beautiful testimony of God's redeeming love and restoration. The imagery of the shards of glass remind us all of things we too can carry around in our broken mirrors.

Reading Sugar's story helps us to not only relate but also reflect upon and ultimately examine our own lives and the vulnerable areas that we need to allow God to rebuild and repair. You will be so inspired by *Shattered Mirror* that you too will be ready to hand over all your shattered pieces to God so you see the real reflection and beauty in your own life that only God, the Master Restorer, can Restore.

Michelle Bollom
Ordained Minister & Founder Restored Ministries

Life.....Fragments....Broken Pieces...Puzzled....WHY??? Take a moment to Reflect! Do we throw it away once life is broken or try to put it back together again? Is it worth it? Really! *Shattered Mirror* is allowing us to journey through the life of Author Trask and Mirror Image our own Life Reflections. One may ask themselves "Can I be mended from the pain of my past?

Author Dr. Sugar Trask's book *Shattered Mirror* is providing the tools step by step how to break free from the past and walking you over to a Victorious Lifestyle of living! Grab hold to the Rope of Hope as the lifeline is being tossed out. "Break the Silence" and Breakthrough those Images of Life that want to keep you bound and experience your freedom through this book! Author Dr. Sugar Trask is keeping it real, allowing a Peek a Boo Moment through the Mirror of Life Images!

As you read the words in this book: Relax, Relate & Release so you can breathe PEACE! Let the Healing begin from the Inside Out! "Shattered Mirror" of Life Despairs!

Life...Fragments of Broken Pieces ...Puzzled!! Stand Up! Rise Up! Get your Life Back on Track from one look at Author Dr. Sugar Trask's *Shattered Mirror* and experience your FREEDOM! Now walk in Victory!

Lady Diana Flagg
CEO, Women Empowerment Bookclub
Restore, Rebirth & Peace
Newark, NJ

Knowing Dr. Trask as well as I do, it is amazing that she has even survived to tell the tale of her history. Most people would be bitter and resentful, unwilling to help another after surviving such tragedy. However, that is just most people, and not Dr. Sugar Trask!

Sugar has an enormous heart to help people. Her love pours out, and her "mercy-bone" is extremely evident when she ministers. And minister she does! She pours out both her heart, and the Father's heart, on the pages of this book, ministering to all who read it. I am sure that this memoir of Dr. Trask's healing will impact your life in some way as she ministers to you through it.

There are very few people in today's culture in America that will not be touched in some way by this insightful and deeply thoughtful self-examination. Most people are following in Dr. Trask's footsteps, on their way out of the trap of drugs and alcohol, or knows someone who is fighting a similar battle. This story can be used as a road map to "get-out" of many harmful situations that Dr. Trask has endured and survived. She now teaches others how to do the same. Enjoy the journey!

Edie Bayer
Author, Minister, Prophet, Publisher

Table of Contents

~~~~~~~~~~~~~~~~~~~~~~~~~~~~~~~~

Introduction

~~~~~~~~~~~~~~~~~~~~~~~~~~~~~~~~~

Shattered Mirror on the wall
Who's the fairest of them all
As I gaze upon the floor
A shattered mirror, my life's no more
Some pieces yet still in the frame
The broken years, I was to blame
Searching, looking, never to find
Still in awe, I didn't lose my mind
I share with you my broken beginnings
My testimony speaks of God's great ending.

Have you ever dropped a mirror that shattered into pieces? Did you notice how some of those pieces remained larger while others were smaller? When you picked the mirror up from the floor, did the broken pieces begin to fall again? This is a direct correlation to my life. I had an ideal image of what my life was supposed to look like with so many hopes, dreams and visions for my future.

One day, I was looking in the mirror. The truth of who I had become caused my mental mirror to fall and the pieces of my life shatter. There were just enough pieces still in place for me to deceive myself into wearing a distorted mask to hide my tainted truth.

Are you covering up your distorted truth? Do you see the shattered pieces of your life, but feel they cannot be salvaged? *Shattered Mirror* is for the individual seeking to put the broken pieces of their life back together again. My pieces were beyond shattered. I had allowed the enemy to take the tiniest bits of my life and grind them into nothing. That is how I felt.

God reminded me that He knitted me in my mother's womb and knew me before I was born. I began to seek God for the plans that He had for me. I knew that I didn't have the power to renew my broken life and make it new. However, God did! He is the Potter and I am the clay. I had to allow God to melt my stony heart and to reshape it on His Potter's wheel.

In this Introduction to my life, I have been led to share the first seventeen years of my journey. As the years of my life progressed and regressed, yes, I was stressed. But in the end, I am so blessed!

Writing this book increased my level of confidence in my Father. As I began to pour out the pains of my past, I became self-aware of His abundant overflowing grace. I began to reflect on the joy and the accelerated blessings that God had planned for my life so long ago.

This book has given me the opportunity to be transparent

which leaves me open and vulnerable, but it is all to the glory of God. I overcame the enemy by the blood of the Lamb and by the word of my testimony, which is why I am sharing my shattered experience with you.

Prayerfully, my testimony will reveal some shattered pieces in your mirror and lead you to God who is your Healer also. You will become accountable to the wisdom that is required to seek healing and deliverance for your own life journey.

My life has truly been one of despair. I have gone from hell to heaven, from gloom to glory, from eternal death to eternal life where I am now living in the fullness of Jesus Christ. The experience of revisiting my life has helped me to heal and I am convinced that if God can do it for me, He can also do it for you.

It has been amazing to witness the Holy Spirit's leading while writing this book. I asked God long ago if the *Shattered Mirror* would one day be made whole. He gently replied, "All things are possible to him who believes." I believe!

Enjoy reading the story of my life through the series of the *Shattered Mirror*!

Chapter One

~~~~~~~~~~~~~~~~~~~~~~~~~~~~~~~

The Smell of Death

Have you ever considered what it took to get you here? Yes, we know that two people came together intimately; the egg and the sperm connected and conception took place. But, have you ever realized that at the moment of conception, the enemy began plotting against your life? In reality, an innocent seed that could do no harm posed a serious threat to the enemy.

As I reflect back over my life, I now understand that the enemy knew more about me than I knew about myself. He had a glimpse into the future of the visions, dreams and goals that God implanted into my soul and he was determined to destroy everything about me.

I am reminded of Romans 8:28, which says, *"All things work together for good to them that love God, to them who are the called according to his purpose."*

Did you read the part that said, "...the called?" Well, that is me, Sugar, because God called me from my mother's womb. A womb that did not want to receive me. A womb that wanted to reject me even before I knew what being rejected felt like. On February 3, 1954, my mother, Rose Givens, walked into Parkland Hospital in Dallas, Texas, expecting to give birth to a bouncing baby girl. Already having birthed two children, she was convinced that she would have another Cesarean like she had had with my siblings. The doctor examined my mother to see how much she had dilated. After the examination, the doctor delivered the gut-wrenching news that I was, in fact, stillborn.

None of this made sense because my mother was a healthy 21-year-old woman who had already delivered two healthy children. The doctor told my mother there was nothing they could do for her or her baby. They packed her with gauze and gave her a shot that would cause the fetus, me, to be aborted within six days. This fact is strategic because on the sixth day God made man.

After she passed the fetus, she was told, she needed to return to the hospital to undergo a surgical procedure to clean out the afterbirth from her womb. But God! What the enemy meant for bad, God used for His glory!

My grandmother took my mother home to deal with the overwhelming pain of losing a child that she had carried for nine months. Minute by minute, hour after hour she waited in anguish for this nightmare to be over. Can you imagine the stress I underwent as an unborn baby, the feelings of abandonment, unworthiness and loneliness that I felt lying in all of the gunk that was causing my mother to be ill? Was she convinced that she had to get rid of this baby that was making her sick? Women can die during childbirth. Did she think she would die as well?

I know today that she didn't say those words because she believed that the doctors were wrong. She believed her baby was going to be fine and healthy by the grace of God.

Keep in mind that this was in 1954 when segregation was still prevalent. My mother was a 21- year-old, unwed and unemployed Negro woman with two other children. She had to enter the hospital through the back door, which speaks volumes about her situation.

As the days passed, my mother continued a downward spiral. She developed a horrible smell from the packing in her vagina. When my mother was convinced that she was dying, she reached out to her father who was living in Oklahoma. Her father drove down to Dallas to get her and take her back to Oklahoma.

When they got to Shawnee, my grandfather stopped at the nearest hospital. When he got my mother in the door, he explained that the Dallas hospital intended to let her die along with her supposedly dead baby.

When I think about this, I am reminded of the story of Lazarus who had been dead for four days and was already stinking. Oh, but when Jesus showed up, He called Lazarus by name and commanded him to come forth. The people were astounded when the corpse walked out of the tomb.

As I lay nestled in my mother's womb with the abortion medicine flowing through her bloodstream causing a horrible smell, Jesus showed up in that hospital on February 9, 1954. He declared victory over the enemy and death and commanded that I live.

To this very day, the events of my birth have been puzzling. The Word of God declares that many are called, but few are chosen. I know that I was chosen. I know this because the enemy was determined to kill me before I could even take my first breath. Please don't think that he stopped there. This victory over death only intensified his attacks on my life, my purpose, my future and my destiny through the years.

God had created the preview of my life and once the enemy got a glimpse of the screen, his attacks were intensified. He did his best to shatter my reflection in that mirror. He wanted me to live a confused life. He pushed me to portray the role of a rejected soul in search for love in all the wrong places.

There are so many pieces to this shattered mirror that I call my life and I made every attempt to put the pieces together. The more that I attempted to see my reflection in the mirror, the more shattered and distorted my reflection became.

My loving Father God had a plan for my life. He saw

my ups and my downs, my ins and my outs. I was the one who had to catch up to my potential that God knew and had planned. My life was going to be rough, but it was going to work out for my good. It was all part of God's master plan.

NO ONE can foil His plans. If He said it, He is going to do it. If He planned it, it is going to happen. I guess the enemy hasn't learned this lesson quite yet because he continues to make every attempt to steal, kill and destroy God's people. But I am a living witness that God always has the last say.

Brace yourself because the story is just beginning. You are about to journey with me through the shattered pieces of my life.

Shattered Mirror

Journal Your Shattered Moments

(Deuteronomy 32:39 NKJV) 'Now see that I, even I, am He, And there is no God besides Me; I kill and I make alive; I wound and I heal; Nor is there any who can deliver from My hand.

Chapter Two

~~~~~~~~~~~~~~~~~~~~~~~~~~~~~~

Miracles and Mishaps

mir·a·cle ['mirǝk(ǝ)l]

NOUN

A surprising and welcome event that is not explicable by natural or scientific laws and is therefore considered to be ***the work of a divine agency.***

"The work of a divine agency!" WOW! What a wonderful way to explain the unimaginable signs and wonders that God performs in the earth! I can honestly say that I am a miracle child and, from what you have already read, I am sure you agree. I mean, let's be real.

Using scientific logic, I was supposed to be lying dead inside of my mother, not preparing to be born. My almighty Father hid me under the shadow of His wings. He blocked the abortion medicine from affecting any part of me. I am here today to tell you about the glory of God. I am here today to say my God is sovereign. No matter how it looked, He was in control.

Now, don't get me wrong. Even though the enemy lost the battle to kill me before I was born, he didn't just give up. He had an agenda in mind that included killing Shelia by any means necessary.

I certainly had no clue that the enemy had a hit out on me. I didn't understand that my birth alone put a major glitch in his plans. I had no idea that God had equipped me for His glory and that the enemy was trying to taint my story. None of this would register until much later in my life.

I never had the pleasure of meeting my biological father, but I have pictures of him. Every time I look in the mirror, I see his face and his full lips. Each time that I look at my hands, I know where my large hands came from. More than anything, I understand that God doesn't make mistakes. There was a reason for my father's absence from my life. I do know that he was a military man who traveled the world. One fateful day, he made a drastic mistake that cost him his freedom and cast him into jail for over twenty years.

There was something missing in my life and I could never quite put my hands on it. Just like a mirror that slips from your hand and falls to the floor, it doesn't break the first time. You get excited as you remember the old wives tale that says the individual who breaks a mirror will have bad luck. But, what if the mirror continues to fall time after time? Eventually, that mirror will break and become useless.

My life was beginning to look as if the enemy had

permission to pick me up and drop me at will hoping I would soon shatter into nothing. I was bumped and shoved, bruised and broken; however, my God knew and kept my heart close to His.

After my birth, my mother moved my older brother, sister and me to Shawnee, Oklahoma to live. Everything was quiet for many months. Then the excitement started again.

Picture a child who is trusting and friendly. Because children don't see good and evil, everything to a child seems innocent. One beautiful day, mom goes to work and I am having fun playing with my siblings.

Suddenly, someone bursts into the house, grabs the three of us, a few of our belongings and rushes us back out of the house. Confusion, tears, and fear take over the scene. Just imagine the torment of being taken away from your family, wondering if you would ever see them again.

Or does it make a difference when the kidnapper is a relative? Should it be considered something as harsh as kidnapping? I don't know your answer, but my mother considered it kidnapping when my Aunt Boogie arrived unannounced to take the three of us away from Mom while she was at work.

My mother's sister, Aunt Boogie, had ridden on a train for three days from Tranquility, California to find us in

Shawnee, Oklahoma. The police would consider her actions premeditated kidnapping because she had three whole days to contemplate her idea.

You may be thinking she had to be mentally ill, but that was not the case. My dear Great Aunt was convinced that she could take better care of us than my young, unwed 21-year-old mother could. Once she had gathered us and a few of our things together, she ushered us back to the train for the long ride to her home in Tranquility.

My aunt may have lived in a place called Tranquility, which means "calm and serene", but there was nothing calm and serene about what she was doing. I can only imagine the agony my mother must have experienced when she walked through the door to find us missing without a trace. I was only eighteen months old at the time.

Aunt Boogie did send a telegram to inform my mother that she had us and that we were fine. I don't know what she was on, but did she really expect my mother to just say, "OK" and go on about her business?

As soon as my mother received the telegram, she contacted her friend, Herman, in Dallas, to take her to Tranquility. They didn't take the train, they drove. My mother is very feisty so I can imagine her during this unwarranted road trip. He certainly had his hands full to keep her under control while she worried about her babies.

My mother was a kind and gentle woman. She was very nurturing and loving. However, when it came to her kids, she was like a mama bear if they were getting hurt in any way.

When my mother and Herman arrived in Tranquility, they started asking around the neighborhood if anyone had seen Aunt Boogie with three small kids. Quite naturally, the neighbors told them that Aunt Boogey had "left to get her kids", as if we actually belonged to her.

Aunt Boogie's husband was home watching us that day. We were happily playing together when excitement reared its ugly head once again. My mother and Herman arrived in another whirlwind of activity, grabbed our things and rushed us out the door and into their car. While Aunt Boogie was at work, we all made a clean get-a-way. We were back on the road in no time, heading back home to Oklahoma.

You would think with all that I had to experience to get here that I would get a break from drama, but it was honestly just beginning. The enemy had marked me and if he could not physically kill me, he was going to try psychological assassination.

Maybe you can relate to being under attack mentally. I have always heard that a mind is a terrible thing to waste. Well, does that apply when your mind is under attack?

Thoughts govern how we live our lives, day to day. When thoughts are not aligned with God's thoughts, a life can become unbearable.

I got a glimpse of unbearable living at a very early age and there was nothing within my power that I could do to stop it. I had to learn how to play with the cards that I was dealt. I did not receive a good hand at all. I wanted so much to have the card dealer turn His head while I snuck my cards back in the deck to grab some others, but that wasn't going to work.

My life would go on as planned by the almighty God with many detours and pits ahead. This is going to be a bumpy ride as you continue to travel through this journey of my challenging life adventures. A life filled with plenty of miracles and mishaps!

Shattered Mirror

Journal Your Shattered Moments

Chapter Three

~~~~~~~~~~~~~~~~~~~~~~~~~~~~~~~~~

Building on a Weak Foundation

"You can't build a great building on a weak foundation. You must have a solid foundation if you're going to have a strong superstructure." - Gordon B. Hinckley

After the kidnapping event, my mother, Herman, my siblings and I stayed in Shawnee for about three months before moving to Minneapolis, Minnesota. My mother married Herman and we all lived in a comfortable home on 28th Avenue near the train tracks. We even had a dog-named Lucky.

The first two years of my life appeared to be turbulent, but eventually things started to get better, or so I thought. I mentioned that we lived near the train track. One day, a train hit a car. The mangled metal and glass landed flat smack dab in the middle of our yard. Can you imagine the scene? Torn bodies on the ground, screaming people, and gruesome bloody body parts surrounded me as I stood there in the midst of it all. I had no clue that one day I would work in a funeral home tenderly caring for bodies of newly departed souls.

There were many instances that I can recall growing up

that I now understand were foundational. As a child, I was always very helpful and not afraid to take a risk. My level of curiosity was extreme.

I recall my sister, Valerie, closing her hand in the car door. This was an excruciating pain that I wouldn't wish on my worst enemy. To see her hand deformed and bleeding... oh, there was so much blood! For some reason I knew what to do. As fast as I could, I ran to the kitchen, filled a bag with ice and quickly put her hand in it.

In the midst of my playing "Nurse Shelia" to my sister, our mother was in a panic hysterically running back and forth through the house trying to get her to the hospital. I did not understand at that time how I knew what to do, but today I understand that God was forming and molding me for my future. He was creating me to be a spiritual "first responder".

My family moved from 28th Avenue to a bigger house on 17th Avenue. The woman who lived next door was from Germany. Apparently, she did not like people who were not the same shade of color as she was.

One day there was a knock at the door. When we opened the door, the gentleman on our doorstep said there had been an accident. When we walked outside, we saw green paint all over my mother's brand new black Buick. Our racist neighbor had shown her true colors.

This was the craziest thing I had ever seen, but that was life during that time. We learned how to take the crooked with the straight. This was my first true introduction to racism.

My grandmother came to live with us in the new house. She was no longer with my grandpa who had rescued my mother during her pregnancy. She had remarried. She and her new husband were both alcoholics. Their arrival in my life proved to be my introduction to alcoholism.

One day, in the midst of a drunken stupor, Granny's husband got physical with her. This was a shock to me because I had never witnessed a man putting his hands on a woman in that manner. Well, Granny didn't play around. She pulled out a straight razor. As much as she wanted to slice his throat, she gave him a warning and only sliced his tie instead. I was so glad because I didn't want to visit Granny in the big house.

My stepfather intervened by picking up Granny's husband and throwing him out the back door. These were some wild times, but they were teaching me a lot about life. I just didn't know it at the time.

I can recall my first introduction to two people having intercourse. As a little girl, I would help my stepfather clean the church on Saturdays. He was a very prestigious leader in the church who served as a deacon, on the trustee board, as a chairman and also as the church custodian.

My brother and I would go with him to clean the church. I was always assigned to trash duty. Well, one day I encountered more than my young little eyes should have seen.

Two of the church leaders were getting busy in one of the offices. I don't mean getting busy praying either. I had enough sense to walk away and never say anything. Ironically, that Christmas I received very nice gifts from both of the individuals. Receiving gifts for secrecy was to become a growing trend in my life.

We lived in a very nice home. My mother and stepfather worked very hard to provide the best for us. We thought we were normal especially compared to others who lived around us. I will never forget our neighbors who lived across the street.

Their house reminded me of the nursery rhyme, "There Was an Old Woman Who Lived in a Shoe." There were so many kids in that one house! It seemed they were everywhere causing excitement night and day!

One of the kids had a birthday party and my siblings and I were invited. When we went over for the party, we saw a weird looking cake on the table. The cake had frosting on it, but the cake certainly wasn't Duncan Hines, it was cornbread. I am not criticizing the less fortunate, but this was crazy. How can you eat ice cream with cornbread?

We just joined in the party and ate what was served! We opened our mouths and did it! We loved it! We had the best time that day.

Now, I understand that the family was very dysfunctional, but they appeared to be happy. They were happier than my family who seemed to have everything. Do not get me wrong, they did fight at times and there was always something interesting going on across the street. I would take food over to them, because that cornbread cake just stuck with me. This experience also helped to build a foundation of giving that would propel me into a life of blessings.

God knew exactly what I needed to become His Shelia. He knew the very things that would shape my character to His design and will. He knew what would develop integrity, faith, confidence and willpower within me.

We may not agree with the various things that God allows in our lives to create our foundations but His Word doesn't lie. When He said, ALL works out for our good, I am a living witness that it ALL works out in the end.

Did I always believe this? Of course not! Too many bad things happened throughout my life that seemed totally unfair.

Have you ever found yourself wishing that you could start life all over again? If you could take everything that you have learned in life and start over, do you think better or different circumstances would arise? These are questions that I ask my sixty-three-year-old self after looking back at all that life has thrown my way.

Don't get me wrong, I am truly grateful and forever thankful to God that He chose to deliver and set me free. But I must admit that my life started on a very weak, distorted foundation.

At an early age, I began to form certain habits and one of them was sucking my fingers. I found so much comfort in my middle and ring fingers. Maybe it was a coping mechanism, but no matter the reason, I couldn't stop doing it. My parents had an issue with this behavior, and took it upon themselves to stop me from doing it. Today, their method of prevention would be considered ABUSE!

I was tortured by the smell of my stepfather's feet. He had the worst smelling feet which would often bleed and peel. They were just disgusting! Even when he left his shoes outside, the smell would still smother us on the inside of the house.

In an attempt to stop my finger sucking, my mother doused my hands with hot sauce and taped my fingers together. I am sure this is the reason that I can tolerate very hot peppers today. The worst punishment of all was taping my stepfather's funky socks to my hands. This was child abuse in its rarest form. I would have probably preferred to get beat with an extension cord buck naked, than to be tortured by the constant smell of this man's feet.

This planted a very negative seed on the inside of me. It was torture! Understand that when seeds are planted, they eventually grow. What they grow into is up to the person that is nurturing the seed, but there was nothing nurturing about this. I am sure they meant well because they didn't want me to have buckteeth or get sick from sucking on germs. However, it planted something deep within my soul alongside many other negative things that were to come.

In addition to my finger issues, I was a bed wetter. There were a number of things going on with me that stemmed from a deeper place, but no one was looking at it that way.

As you can see, there was a lot going on in my life during those early years that are critical to a child's mental, physical, spiritual and emotional development. There was a massive hole forming in my soul and at that time, I didn't understand why. I thought I was normal, but I was far from normal. My choices and decisions throughout life were going to sound the alarm to this fact.

I was on an emotional roller coaster and didn't even

know how I got on the ride. Things were happening to me that were out of my control and I was learning at an early age to mask my pain. My foundation was being built on lies, pain and trauma. Eventually, once the house was completely built, it was destined to come tumbling down.

Shattered Mirror

Journal Your Shattered Moments

(Psalms 6:2 NKJV) Have mercy on me, O LORD, for I am weak; O LORD, heal me, for my bones are troubled.

Chapter Four

~~~~~~~~~~~~~~~~~~~~~~~~~~~~~~~~~~

"A Contaminated Innocence"

I often hear people talk about how much fun they had in elementary school. They talk about the games they played, the stories they remember the teachers reading and the best class of all was always recess. I have these memories as well, but I also have bad memories of those days in elementary school.

I loved Mrs. Thompson, my third grade teacher, even though she was plush and cuddly. She reminded me of an old grandmother because of the way that she hugged me. I recall she had a peculiar smell that I could never quite identify. Today, I realize she was hitting the flask before coming to class. Yes, fluffy Mrs. Thompson was an alcoholic. The examples that were presented to me at an early age were just bizarre, but God!

As I stated in the last chapter, I was a "bed wetter." We had a daily naptime at school. When I would awaken, I would be wet. My mother always packed extra clothes for me, but nothing took away from the fact that I was teased for my "accidents."

New seeds of rejection and low self-esteem were planted in my soul. Kids were so cruel. In most instances, they didn't know any better, but it still hurt. I had to deal with being taunted by my peers, being called "pissy Shelia" and other horrible names.

One day we had a substitute teacher who was not familiar with my situation. During naptime, I wet myself. Even though I tried to tell her that I had a change of clothes, she would not allow me to change. There was no legitimate excuse for her actions. She made me stand during the remainder of the class and sent me home in soiled clothing. Can you imagine how humiliating this was?

I was the tallest in my class. I was the biggest in my class. I had the largest hands in my class. To top it all off, I had a bladder and a finger sucking problem. I felt the odds were stacked against me. This was way too much for one child to handle, or was it? Because the saying goes, "What doesn't kill you only makes you stronger!"

My mother was furious when I arrived home in soiled clothes and she didn't play around. I don't know who she punched in the face or what nasty words she gave that school, but I didn't have any more problems after the issue with the substitute teacher. Everyone in the school knew not to mess with Shelia after that.

During that era, if you were left handed, the teachers would "pop" your left hand with a ruler to make you write with your right hand. I am still a leftie because they knew not to pop me.

Yet, I still had to deal with the frequent teasing. There were times when the kids would take my soiled clothes from my bag and throw them around to others. It was very hard being the tallest in the class and wetting my clothes. When we had events at school, I was always the last in line because I was the tallest.

Even if we were in alphabetical order, I still had to be at the end of the line and my last name started with an "H." I was called stupid because kids thought that I was supposed to be in the sixth grade and flunked because I was so tall. They stole my lunch nearly every day.

The torture went on and on but eventually I got over it. I learned to have tough skin. I understood that it would eventually be over one day. I found solace in doing well in my schoolwork, keeping up with my homework and helping to clean the black board and erasers after school. Then I was called the "teacher's pet," but who cared? I certainly didn't. There were too many other things going on behind the scenes.

I have heard my entire life that parents are to train up their children in the fear and admonition of the Lord. What happens when one parent is training and another parent is destroying? What happens when one parent is loving you and embracing you the way that a parent should and the other is touching you and violating you in ways that a parent never should?

Molestation is real and I can say that from personal experience. At a very early age, I was molested and violated by my stepfather. The sad thing about it is, I didn't even know that it was wrong. As a child, you trust your parents and you never imagine in your wildest dreams that they would do anything to harm you. Therefore, I was under the impression that what was being done to me was normal. I was supposed to like it and never say anything to anyone under any circumstances. What he did to me was a secret. This was my introduction to sex and money. I was given special attention as well as very nice presents in exchange for my silence.

By the time I entered elementary school, we had moved to Portland Avenue and Clinton Elementary was located off Fourth Avenue. Since I lived within walking distance, I was allowed to go home for lunch. When I would arrive home, my stepfather would be there taking a lunch break and my mother would be at work.

My stepfather cooked the most amazing hamburgers, but these burgers came at an alarming cost... my childhood innocence, which was very dear and precious to this little girl. My stepfather would sit me on his lap and put his hands under my dress to fondle my girly parts and kiss me on the mouth. Once he was done, he would get up from the table, drop the plates in the sink and head back to work.

Other times he would come into my room at night and bring a wet towel. I thought he would clean me up because I would be wet from wetting the bed. In reality, the towel was to clean himself after masturbating while fondling me.

Here we go with the seeds again. First, it was verbal abuse, then rejection and low self-esteem and now the seeds of self-hatred and fear. Quite naturally, he was like any other child molester. He always cautioned me not to tell anyone or else. This was supposed to be our little secret that no one was supposed to know about. Even though this was being done *to* me against my will, self-hatred was setting in. I would look in the mirror and didn't really know who or what I was looking at. Why was all of this happening to me?

Darkness started to invade my mind. When I should have been running in the streets, smelling flowers and blossoming into a beautiful young woman, instead, I was evolving into a young girl filled with pain. A young girl whose soul was being tormented. A young girl whose body was being violated. A young girl who was learning at an early age not to trust and not to love. I was building up walls to keep the predators out, but somehow, they kept knocking my walls down.

Eventually, I fought back, but I kept getting beat down. I was the one being violated. Instead of loving myself, I began to hurt myself even more.

As time went on, I continued growing. I was bigger than everyone else my age. I was even bigger than my mother and my sister. In the sixth grade, I was around 160 pounds, wearing a size nine shoe, size 16 clothes and a 36B in bras.

Between the third and sixth grades, I was molested by friends who would come by the house to visit my siblings. I didn't understand. I know I didn't have a sign on my forehead that read, "Hey, my name is Shelia and I want to have sex!" They knew I was the baby sister. Apparently, it didn't matter because of my size.

I was in a place of total shame and I still didn't have any idea that what was happening to me was very wrong. I was under the assumption that it was right, but just a secret. I believed I belonged to a secret society.

Even though I was having a hard time in school, I found myself liking boys and my first crush was David Brown. He would carry my books and we would kiss all the time.

I had a friend named Mary whose mother was extremely obese and their house was just nasty. It always appeared as if a tornado hit the entire house. Mary had a brother who was also forcing me into dark places to have sex in their attic.

Mary and I went to a sleepover one night and the enemy was finally exposed. For the years that I was being molested, I didn't have any words to describe what was happening to me. I just knew I was being touched, kissed and poked. During the sleepover, one of the girls talked about one of our peers named Elizabeth who had been raped.

While they discussed the details of what had happened, I was sitting there thinking that "this" happens to me all the time. Finally, I could put a name on it and I realized that "it" was very wrong. The gifts I received for this violation and the vows to silence were making sense. Elizabeth had to leave school and stay with her grandmother because her father had been caught in bed with her.

Well, "this" had been happening to me for years. This startling discovery caused me to sink into deeper despair. I didn't want to be forced to leave my mother and my siblings because of other people's issues with darkness. I couldn't go anywhere to stay with Granny because she was living with us. I couldn't say anything because I was sworn to silence.

There was one person I knew who would protect me, but I also knew she really was crazy. If I told her what had been going on, I had no idea what the outcome would have been. I chose to bear the pain alone in silence.

Eventually, I found a coping mechanism that would temporally shield me from the pain. It would mask the hurt, the tension and the embarrassment. Something that was supposed to be temporary eventually had a long-lasting effect on my future.

Keep reading and you will soon discover the demons that I allowed to enter and to dwell within me for many years.

Shattered Mirror

Journal Your Shattered Moments

_____

_____

_____

_____

_____

_____

_____

_____

_____

(Psalms 107:20 NKJV) He sent His word and healed them, And delivered them from their destructions.

Chapter Five

~~~~~~~~~~~~~~~~~~~~~~~~~~~~~~~

"The Dope Helped Me Cope"

Bryant Junior High, those were the days! We had a teacher named Mrs. Johnson who had one brown eye and one blue eye. It sounds weird, but imagine seeing her every day. She was a cool teacher, but I always seemed to get the teachers who had some form of addiction. Mrs. Thompson was an alcoholic and Mrs. Johnson kept a fat bottle of pills in her desk drawer. She had a variety of downers, uppers and other pills to keep her calm.

One day, we had a substitute teacher. Mrs. Johnson hadn't taken her pills home so I snuck some out of a bottle. I had no idea what the pills would do to me, but I popped one in my mouth and quickly swallowed it. After about a half hour, I began to get very sluggish. I was feeling relaxed and sleepy to the point that I was falling asleep in class. I wasn't sure what the pills were for, but this was the open door to my becoming a pharmaceutical junkie.

During that time, there was a diet pill called "Black Molly" that was very popular. It was "speed". It would speed up your speech, your energy and cause a rush for hours. It wasn't long before I was popping "downers" and "uppers" -- the street terms for drug use. The other girls were popping pills also and smoking cigarettes. Somehow, I never got interested in smoking cigarettes.

During this time, I was getting older but my size hadn't changed. My stepfather was still sneaking into my room to masturbate while fondling me. As the school year continued, my habit of popping diet pills increased to camouflage the pain. They made me feel good and became very addictive.

I didn't know that I had planted seeds of self-sabotage and suicide. I was setting myself up for an early grave. Because the illicit drugs were damaging my body and increasing my heart rate, I could have died because of the abuse. But God!

My friends and I were having a good time. We went to parties and spiked the punch. Now I was introduced to drinking alcohol.

In junior high, I was able to walk to school by myself. The girls I was hanging with should have been called, "trouble" and "more trouble." They both had older and younger siblings and lived in dysfunctional households. Thankfully, I was no longer the only one standing in the back row for class pictures. I was starting to blend in with the other girls.

Helen's older brothers would play hooky from school to smoke weed and drink. They would corner us and make us pull down our pants or they would pull down theirs and show us their private parts. We would run out of the house as fast as we could to get away.

We became little rebels back then and nothing was going to stop us. But even having someone to hang with never stopped the pain that I was feeling on the inside...the pain of being dragged into a basement or secluded dark corner by a childhood friend or uncle.

I began to have thoughts of killing myself to escape the pain, but I didn't know it was called suicide. I just knew that I wanted to die. I felt death would be better than what I faced each and every day. I knew that people had killed themselves by way of carbon monoxide or from taking a bunch of pills. A girl at our school had slashed her wrists and a boy in the ninth grade had hung himself.

I just wanted the pain to leave because the pills just got me high and made my world go faster. They couldn't shut off my brain and stop the constant images of this boy's private parts or that man rubbing his body against mine. The movie of my past kept playing over and over again.

I had a friend named Sharon who also had a dysfunctional family. I was visiting her one day and heard her sister telling her mom that she was pregnant and that she had been burnt. I thought she had been burned with an iron or with fire, but she was referring to a venereal disease.

The guy that she was sleeping with had a sexually transmitted disease. Another scene…another show…more drama…just drama all the time.

The Word of God tells us to be wary of wolves in sheep's clothing. Well, this Word should be treasured and followed. Unfortunately, I ignored that lesson too often.

In spite of how I felt, I made sure that I went to school every day. Getting my education was very important. Every morning, we had to pass the high school in order to get to the junior high.

One day, when Sharon and I were walking to school, a guy was standing outside and he was every bit of fine. The young fellow's name was Al. He called Sharon over and told her to bring me with her. Because of my tainted past with boys who had no parental supervision, I instantly thought I was going to be dragged into another house to have sex. He asked her for my name and she told him.

He said, "I know your mother, Rose. She plays golf with my mother. You live down there on Portland. I have met your brother, but never you or your sister. It was nice meeting you, Shelia."

Sharon and I went on our way. I was in heaven. I daydreamed about him all day and all night.

The next day I was heading to Sharon's house to pick her up for school and I had to pass Al's house. He was standing outside. When he saw me, he said, "Good morning." He then asked me to stop by his house after school. He claimed it was just to talk because he wasn't into the other stuff.

A wolf in sheep's clothing and I ignored the thought! Quite naturally, I was in "Al" la la land all day, waiting for the bell to ring in dire anticipation of what Mr. Al wanted. During lunch, Sharon told me some interesting things about this person named Al. She explained how he had been "burnt" and that he had "burnt" others. I was sitting there hoping he was OK because I didn't understand that she was talking about a venereal disease like gonorrhea.

The bell finally rang and I was overly excited to get to Al's house. When I arrived, he offered me a drink and there was a picture of his mother and my mother golfing on the table. Nothing happened that day, but that doesn't mean that he wasn't plotting.

Months went by and the day finally came when he invited me to come in and go upstairs. He wanted to show me something. He wanted to show me something all right! His mother was away at a golf tournament so again, I was in a house with no parental supervision and that usually meant sex.

Sharon tried to warn me about him, but I was so lost in orbit that I couldn't believe that he would outright give me a disease like VD. I gave into him and we slept together.

Remember, several times I have stated wolf in sheep's clothing. The sole purpose of the disguise is to trick the prey into believing that you are something that you are not. When his "prey" gets comfortable and lets their guard down, the wolf will expose himself and then attack.

This is how I felt when I found out that I contracted the same venereal disease that Sharon had warned me about. I felt so stupid because I was mesmerized by his looks and had ignored the facts. My life had already been filled with one devastating blow after another and now this. The enemy had attacked again.

When I finally thought that I had found something or someone that I loved and who loved me, BAM, I was hit by a Mack-10 truck right in the middle of my heart. I didn't know how I was going to bounce back from that.

Molestation, rape, sexual abuse, drugs, alcohol, suicidal thoughts, rejection, abandonment, low self-esteem and self-sabotage were demon hunters because the enemy was on me like "white on rice" and he was not letting go. The enemy had put a hit out on my life. He called in all of the demon hunters and put a nice reward out for whichever one could kill me first. But God!

Shattered Mirror

Journal Your Shattered Moments

(Hosea 14:4 NKJV) "I will heal their backsliding, I will love them freely, For My anger has turned away from him.

Chapter Six

~~~~~~~~~~~~~~~~~~~~~~~~~~~~

The Wolf Exposed

I am sure you recall the story of Little Red Riding Hood. The big bad wolf tried to disguise himself as Little Red Riding Hood's Granny. He was hungry and wanted to eat her and what she carried in her basket. The story says he stalked Little Red Riding Hood and devised an elaborate plan to take Granny's identity. The big bad wolf almost had Little Red Riding Hood right where he wanted her, but he could not win.

I can relate to this story so easily because the enemy has been disguising himself in various forms my entire life. He came when he tried to kill me at birth. He came in the form of Aunt Boogie. He came in the form of my stepfather. He came in the form of the many boys and men who raped me. He came in the form of Black Mollys and he was about to rear his ugly head once again.

I was so infatuated with Al. Not only did he have good looks, he also played into my childlike fantasies of being more grown than I needed to be. After all, he was in the twelfth grade and I was only in the eighth grade. He was technically a man who saw the size of my body and didn't care about the two digits of my age.

You know you have been there as a teenage girl in junior high. That secret crush you dreamed about. You wrote the guy's name a hundred times in your binder.

Al was no longer a secret crush, it was very much revealed. In fact, more than my heart was revealed. He had consumed all of me. In my gullible state of mind, Al could do no wrong and I was convinced that he loved me.

He was a wolf in sheep's clothing! The enemy will use whoever is open and available for use. He doesn't care how much you love the person. He doesn't care how much it will hurt you or the scars he leaves behind. He doesn't care if you lose your trust in humanity. Death by any means necessary is the enemy's goal.

Proverbs 4:7, says, "In all thy getting, get an understanding." I was getting, but I was lacking in the understanding department. Sharon warned me over and over again! The proof was right in front of my face: the pregnant sister and the other girl who had caught his VD. I still fell for the "okie dokie."

I began my menstrual cycle and it was never regular. One day, I became very ill. I thought it was the flu and my mother took me to General Hospital. They did a pregnancy test and it came back negative…I was not pregnant. Turns out that I had to be hospitalized. I had a very serious infection of my female organs.

Yes, I had contracted the VD from Al. The enemy had finally exposed himself because I didn't have any idea that I had the infection. I must have had it a good while, because of the damage that had been done to my body. I was totally baffled, wondering how Al could do this to me.

My life was on a downward spiral from there. I went to see the gynecologist and I guess the enemy wasn't done because now he was using the doctor. During those examinations, nurses didn't stay in the room. I had to place my feet in those horrible stir-ups with all of my goodies exposed to this man I didn't know. The doctor sat down and inserted the speculum. I was already in pain because there were cysts on my ovaries the size of lemons.

He pushed the speculum in very roughly and then shone a very hot light between my legs. I was very uncomfortable and also concerned because he should have been pressing around for the cysts. He was doing something weird. When I tried to raise my head up, he instantly told me to lie back down. In the midst of sitting up, I was able to clearly see that he was masturbating.

This was becoming a pattern of my demise. Always being told to lie back, shut up, don't say anything, this is our little secret. The funny thing about this incident is that my mother never received a doctor's bill. I wonder why!

Tina Turner sings a song that asks one simple question,

"What does love have to do with it?" I will tell you what, "Nothing", because that is what I felt like when I discovered I had to have surgery. Can you imagine being fifteen years old and having major surgery?

The doctors decided that it was best to go in and scrape the cyst. An intern suggested doing a full hysterectomy. The doctor said, "No". They were using me as a Guinea pig to see how venereal diseases affected African American women. This, in my opinion, was another form of abuse. The hospital was mutilating my body for its own research. My belly would be cut open eight times between the ages of fifteen and twenty-three, which could have been avoided with a hysterectomy at, age 16. This had nothing to do with them trying to save my ovaries so I could possibly have children one day. I was a literal test dummy.

This was a dreary season of my life where the enemy continued to come in various forms. My older brother, Joe, served in Vietnam and when he returned home, he opened the Southside Youth and Young Adult Center that was open to the community. This was a wonderful place for the youth in the community. But, it turned out to be a devil's den for me. That's where I was introduced to the mind altering and hallucinating drugs Acid, THC and Mescaline. These were the drugs of the 70's generation.

The band, Sly Stone had a song, "I Want to Take You

Higher." You can rest assured that Shelia was getting higher and higher and higher. The Portland house became the party house when we were not partying at the Southside Center.

I also had the pleasure of being introduced to another young man who will remain nameless. We shared a bond that was out of this world. Words cannot describe how I felt about him. Al was cute and all, but nothing compared to this special guy. When he entered my life, the sexual abuse from my stepfather ceased and I experienced love for the first time without abuse.

Love, that little four letter word, had become so distorted and twisted that I believed that the only way I could experience love was through pain. I had no idea that the two were not the same and that I could actually smile and it not be fake. I had no idea that someone could touch me in pleasure, instead of torment. I was on cloud nine and I never wanted to come back down to earth.

We shared great times together. He was there for me during some very rough times in my life. Somewhere along the journey, his gentle touch became violent and the love shifted to rage. I was no longer the center of his attention because he began to see other females.

This eventually led to him fathering a child. I tried to press pass the pain and betrayal but I just couldn't do it anymore. It was bad enough that I was hurting myself with the drugs and the choices I was making for my life. I didn't need any more assistance in the pain department. This was a painful experience for me because I had finally known what it was to have someone love and care for me without an ulterior motive. Unfortunately, I also learned that some things are forever and some things are seasonal.

My knight in shining armor turned into someone I no longer recognized. I began to feel as if I would never be healthy, whole and happy.

I am reminded of a song by "The Moments" called "Love on a Two-Way Street." The song says, "I found love on a two-way street and lost it on a lonely highway."

Yes, that was exactly how I felt and I guess that wasn't enough because after my heart failed me, my reproductive system started acting up again. Due to the cysts, fibroids and the excruciating pain I was experiencing, I had to undergo surgery for the second time at the age of sixteen. This surgery removed the cyst, ovary and scar tissue on the left side.

Can you imagine the pain and frustration? My entire childhood had been stolen from me. The days of my life were running together because I had become a full-blown pharmaceutical addict.

What would it take to numb not one pain, not two pains,

but the insurmountable pains of life that were weighing a sister down? I had one of the highest recommended doctors in Minneapolis taking care of me. He prescribed me the good medicine, never realizing that I was using the meds for reasons other than surgical pain.

Those pills had become my way to cope with life. The glass in my "shattered mirror" was no longer breaking in pieces, it felt as if someone was standing on the pieces and grinding them down into the ground. I was slowly but surely becoming non-existent. I was a living being, but I was dying slowly. They could have called me "walking dead Shelia" and I would have answered because that is where I was.

I had finally been awakened to the fact that I was living a dysfunctional life. I was so distracted by the nice house and the things we had growing up, I didn't realize that my life was full of dysfunction. It was everywhere, in my house, in my community, the church, the school and had set up camp in my mind, my heart and my soul. I felt hopeless and began wearing many masks to shield me from the "shattered mirror syndrome."

Shattered Mirror

Journal Your Shattered Moments

_____

_____

_____

_____

_____

_____

_____

_____

_____

_____

(Luke 8:48 NKJV) And He said to her, "Daughter, be of good cheer; your faith h
made you well. Go in peace."

Chapter Seven

~~~~~~~~~~~~~~~~~~~~~~~~~~~~~~

A Darker Path

I have often heard people say that the enemy does not have authority to kill us, but he can push us to kill ourselves. Well, I wanted to kill myself. At first, I was just thinking suicidal thoughts, but now I was ready to act on my thoughts.

My first suicide attempt came in the form of a bottle of Demerol pain meds and a fifth of Vodka. I was tired of bleeding, tired of the mental anguish and the repeated cycles of abuse. I wanted to be free of the mental pain and torture that I was experiencing every day. It is only the grace of God that I am still alive to tell the story. My story is also a witness to the fact that the enemy cannot take my life at will and, apparently, I couldn't either.

Upon entering Nokomis junior high school in Minneapolis, a new demon appeared in the form of cocaine, "that great white devil." I was the only African American student in the school and this elevated me to a completely new level of destruction. I was hanging with a different crowd and their partying and getting high was wilder than anything I had ever imagined.

I would have to assume that God was trying to save me

from the enemy, as well as from myself. It seemed that every time I got into something I shouldn't, I would end up in the hospital dealing with my female organs. Al had really done a number on me with the VD. At the age of seventeen, came surgery number three, which involved the removal of my left Fallopian tube.

Even though I was having these surgeries, nothing seemed to slow me down. My addictions didn't cease because of the surgeries. You would have thought that I would become a virgin Mary with all that was going on in my life, but I wasn't there mentally.

I couldn't seem to see the forest because of the darkness that surrounded me. All I saw was pain, hatred, bitterness, rage, anger and frustration. The only remedy that I wanted was sex, drugs and money. These deceptions had become my strategy for coping with my worthless life.

Every time someone crawled on top of me, I just sank deeper and deeper into a mental grave. I had to become non-existent to myself just to make it day by day. I had to wear a mask to hide who I had allowed myself to become. I was living in a secret world where nobody existed but me. I knew about God, but not even He could fit in my world even though He is omnipresent.

After about nine months, I left Nokomis junior high school and started attending West High School. I was working at Sears & Roebuck and my first car was a midnight blue 64 Buick Riviera with white bucket seats, a gift from my stepfather. I was hanging with a new class of friends which involved a deeper level of abuse. I was all too frequently waking up in hotel rooms, stripped, beaten, robbed, tortured and gang raped.

During high school, I was able to accumulate enough credits from prior summer school attendance which allowed me to graduate in March instead of June with my classmates. For my graduation present, my parents sent me to San Francisco to visit my aunt and her family in the Fillmore District. Was this a drastic mistake!

I was quickly introduced to Haight- Ashbury where the hippies, artists, musicians, dancers, druggies, prostitutes, and homosexuals gathered to indulge in pure darkness. Where we made love, not war! I was able to fit right in because of my past experiences with darkness and demons.

I was supposed to return home after two weeks. Once I was caught in the demon dens, they didn't want to let me go. I couldn't shake the feelings and the experiences I was having and I knew that I couldn't return home in the condition I was in. I had surpassed being a pharmaceutical junkie, I was into free basing, the whole nine yards.

Once my aunt realized what was going on, she said I was no longer welcome at her home. My aunt made it very clear that she didn't want me bringing those demons into her house. This was heartbreaking but I couldn't stop what I was doing.

Since I couldn't go back home, I moved in with one of my cousins. This only opened the door for more demons and more darkness. The Bible says that a warning comes before destruction. God was warning me. I could see the destruction. Yet, I still couldn't stop.

Due to my overindulgence and demonic activities, I was hospitalized once again. Yes, another surgery! This would be surgery number four out of eight. This surgery was to remove cysts on the right side that were the size of a grapefruit and some fibroids. The doctors were still collecting data and giving me experimental drugs that were not working.

All I wanted to do was die. I was tired of being violated physically, verbally and sexually. Even being in the church and knowing God, the emptiness that was inside of me was like a cancer. The only prayer that I had at that time was, "God, please let me die."

I hadn't even touched the surface of womanhood and before I could, it had all been taken away. I was robbed! As a woman, I was created to multiply and replenish the earth, but I would never be able to have any children of my own.

One wrong choice to indulge in a childhood crush had

cost me a lifetime of ever knowing what it would feel like to carry a child in my womb. I would never experience an ultrasound or have my husband place his hand on my belly to feel our baby kick.

I would never have a belly so big I couldn't see my feet or crave weird foods in the middle of the night. I would never have the pleasure of looking into the eyes of someone who looked just like me and was part of me. All because of a stupid crush on one cute boy!

How can you reconnect the pieces of a shattered mirror to make it whole again? You can't! It would give you a distorted view. But I know someone who can.

Jeremiah 18: 3-4 says, *"So I went down to the potter's house, and I saw him working at the wheel. 4 But the pot he was shaping from the clay was marred in his hands; so the potter formed it into another pot, shaping it as seemed best to him."*

The last part of verse four says the potter formed it into another pot, shaping it as seemed best to him. Only God could take my shattered pieces and transform them into a brand-new masterpiece.

No human could convince me that I would be able to bounce back from the gruesome episodes that took place during my developmental years. It was nothing but the grace of God that I was able to survive the constant raping and acts of molestation. It was the favor of God that kept me from overdosing on illicit drugs. It was the mercy of God that protected me during each and every surgery that I had to endure.

"Many are called, but few are chosen." (Matthew 22:14) You have to be able to distinguish between the two. I know today that I was chosen!

I have only shared the first seventeen years of my life with you. If you think this was a wild ride, you have no idea of what is to come.

The weak foundation that I talked about in chapter three was truly just that, weak. My mother was doing her best to ensure that we had the best of everything, but at the cost of my protection. I don't blame her, but I wish I would have opened my mouth and told her what my stepfather was doing to me. Maybe it would have changed things. He was a leader in the church, and yet was plagued by his own demons.

1John 4:4 says, *"Greater is He who is in me, than he that is in the world."* I know this to be a true Word from God and one that I can attest to. It is nothing but the power of God that allowed the wolf to expose himself and be annihilated all at the same time. His weapon was formed against me so many times, but God didn't allow it to prosper. (See Isaiah 54:17.)

Shattered Mirror

Journal Your Shattered Moments

_____

_____

_____

_____

_____

_____

_____

_____

_____

(Luke 6:19 NKJV) And the whole multitude sought to touch Him, for power went out from Him and healed them all.

Chapter Eight

~~~~~~~~~~~~~~~~~~~~~~~~~~~~~~~~~

There Is Hope!

Isaiah 61:7, ESV *Instead of your* **shame** *there shall be a double portion; instead of dishonor they shall rejoice in their lot; therefore in their land they shall possess a double portion; they shall have everlasting joy.*

Shame is a painful feeling of humiliation or distress caused by the consciousness of wrong or foolish behavior. Considering the fact that my name begins with an *"Sh"*, my name should follow "shame" in the dictionary. The definition would read: Shelia - hopeless, bitter, resentful, unworthy, broken, wounded and shattered.

The early years of my life were filled with an excess of mishaps, trials, tests and tribulations. Yet, there is an irony to it all because I am here to tell my story. I am here to encourage you to know that there is hope after dope! I am here to encourage you to know and understand that in our flesh dwells "NO good thing", but we were created by a God who already knew this.

God was so loving that He provided a path to reconcile man back to His side. He even gave us the instructions in His Word so each of us could find our way. (See Romans 7:18) He created a master plan to deliver us from ourselves.

That is what I needed more than anything. I was becoming my own worst enemy. Yes, my stepfather had violated me. Yes, I had been violated and gang raped by many others. Yes, I contracted a venereal disease that turned my life upside down. Yes, that vile infection had a lasting effect on my life and on my future.

In the midst of it all, I made a choice. I chose to allow the enemy full range into my life. I fell for the illusion that I had a right to wallow in my sorrows.

I could have chosen a different path. I could have chosen Jesus each and every time I faced another surgery. I could have chosen the righteous path, but I chose a path of destruction. I chose to play Russian roulette with a life that didn't even belong to me.

With all that was going on, I should have been dead, according to Shelia. But God! Jeremiah 29:11 is a very familiar passage. God says, *"For I know the thoughts that I think toward you, says the LORD, thoughts of peace and not of evil, to give you a future and a hope."*

God knew my future before I was born. He knew yours also. 1 Peter 4:12-19, tells us to rejoice when we encounter fiery trials. Don't think these attacks from the enemy are strange. We are in a battle, but the scripture tells us to rejoice. Being happy in the midst of confusion isn't even logical.

I didn't understand any of God's principles as a child developing into a teenager. I could only glean from what was taking place around me and that was chaos. I was lost in a world of sin so dark that I couldn't even recognize myself. The sin had engulfed me and I was unrecognizable, but God knew my true identity all along. He was simply waiting on the right time to pull me out of the pit and to restore me to His throne of grace and mercy.

The enemy's ultimate plan was to trap me in a place of hopelessness. He wanted me to feel inadequate and incompetent. He used his intimidation and humiliation to devalue my life. He wanted me to agree with his accusations of worthlessness. His ultimate goal was my death!

I can truly say that there is "Hope after dope!" At some point in life, everyone has to make a choice. God tells us we can choose either life or death. (See Deuteronomy 30:19)

At some point in my life, I got tired of myself and I finally chose life. Don't get me wrong, I wanted to die. I wanted to fall asleep and never wake up. However, God had other plans for me. I didn't have a say in my ending and neither do you. At some point, each of us simply have to surrender and give up, because God is eternal and He doesn't grow tired or weary. One day to Him is as a thousand in our world. He will never give up. He will make every attempt for His will to be fulfilled in our lives.

This, my dear friends, is the introduction into my life of despair. It began with a perfect mirror that once displayed an image of a beautiful little girl who was whole, happy and healthy. One day, the enemy released his demon hunters who set out on a journey to shatter the mirror of my life. Through this book, I have exposed the demons that attempted to kill me in my youth.

If you think the first seventeen years were crazy, my story gets ten times worse! To give you a sneak peak of what to expect, I was a full-fledged drug addict for 31 years of my life.

BUT GOD!

"There is Hope"

There is hope all around
There is hope when you are down
There is hope when you can't see your way
There is hope for you today
There is hope when you want to cope
There is hope when you rely on dope
There is hope when you are in pain
There is hope, just call on Jesus' name
There is hope when you see no end
There is hope because God is your friend
There is hope when you have needs
There is hope to help you succeed
There is hope, don't dare give in
There is hope for an expected end.

Shattered Mirror

Journal Your Shattered Moments

.(Hosea 14:4 NKJV) "I will heal their backsliding, I will love them freely, For M
anger has turned away from him.

Shattered Mirror

Journal Your Shattered Moments

(Isaiah 61:1 NKJV) "The Spirit of the Lord GOD is upon Me, Because the LORD has anointed Me To preach good tidings to the poor; He has sent Me to heal the brokenhearted, To proclaim liberty to the captives, And the opening of the prison to those who are bound.

Other Publications

~~~~~~

To purchase other publications
by Dr. Sugar Trask visit
www.scarfree03ministries.com

For speaking opportunities contact

Sugarmarie05@earthlink.net

(409) 789-9631

Dr. "Sugar" teaches on the importance of obtaining and activating the Five Fold Ministry. As an intercessor, prayer warrior, and lover of the almighty God, she makes herself available to minister wherever she is called. She says, "When God says to go, you must go, and what He says to do, you must do."

Her ministry is currently covering four corners of the world by the grace of God and by one prayer at a time. God has appointed, anointed, and prepared her as an international Evangelist to do the work that is so desperately needed. Her passion is to save lost Souls!

She is the founder of W.W.H.O.A. - Women Who Have Overcome Adversities. Evangelist Trask is the author of "God What Now..I Have Prayed!"; "Cookin With Sugarlicious" , "Yes, You Can Cook", "Scriptures to Read and Live By", "Healthy Eating", "Volume One: Scriptures", "Volume Two: Prayers", "Volume Three: Nuggets"; and "Daily Declarations and Decrees."

References

~~~~~~~~~~~~~~~~~~~~~~~~~~~~~~~~~~~~~

1. The Nelson Study Bible NKJV, Radmacher, Editor
2. The Full Life Study Bible - "An International Study Bible for Pentecostal and Charismatic Christians." King James Version, The New Testament-Zondervan Publishing House,1990
3. Encarta ® World English Dictionary ©& (P) 19982005 Microsoft Corporation.

67677923R00052

Made in the USA
Charleston, SC
18 February 2017